IN THE NAME **OF**
ALLAH
THE ALL-COMPASSIONATE, ALL-MERCIFUL

THE GRAVE
Punishment and Blessings

- Title: The Grave - Punishment and Blessings
- Author: Ḥusayn al-'Awayishah
- Translator: Huda Khaṭṭâb
- English Edition 1: 1999
- English Edition 2: 2006
- Layout: IIPH, Riyadh, Saudi Arabia
- Filming & Cover Designing: Samo Press Group

18-The righteous man will sit in his grave unafraid before the questioning, whilst the evil man will sit in his grave utterly terrified.

From 'Â'ishah ( ) who said:

«A Jewish woman came and asked for food at my doorstep, saying, "Feed me, may Allah protect you from the *Fitnah* of the *Dajjâl* and the *Fitnah* of the punishment of the grave." ('Â'ishah) said, "I kept her talking until the Messenger of Allah came, then I asked him, 'O' Messenger of Allah! What is this Jewish woman saying?' I said that she says, 'May Allah protect you from the *Fitnah* of the *Dajjâl* and the *Fitnah* of the punishment of the grave.' 'Â'ishah said, 'Then the Messenger of Allah ( ) stood up and raised his hands (in supplication), seeking refuge with Allah from the *Fitnah* of the *Dajjâl* and the *Fitnah* of the punishment of the grave.' Then he said, 'As for the *Fitnah* of the *Dajjâl*, there has never been a Prophet who did not warn his people against him, but I will tell you something which no Prophet has warned his people about before. He (the *Dajjâl*) is one-eyed, and Allah is not one-eyed; written between his eyes is (the word) *Kâfir*, which every believer will read. As for the *Fitnah* of the grave, (the deceased) will be tested concerning me and asked about me. If he was a righteous man, he will be sat up in his grave, without fear or terror, then he will be asked, 'What did you used to say about Islam? Who was this man who was among you?' He will say, 'Muhammad the Messenger of Allah, who brought the clear signs from Allah, so we believed him.' A hole will be opened for him, through which he will see the Hell-fire, parts of it consuming others. He will be told, 'Look at that which Allah has saved you from.' Then a hole will be opened through which he will see Paradise, with all its luxuries. He will be told, 'This is your place in it.' He will be told, 'You had strong faith, you died with strong faith, and you will be resurrected with strong faith, *in sha' Allah.*

If he was a bad man, he will be sat up in his grave, full of fear and terror, and he will be asked, 'What did you use to say?' He will say, 'I heard the people saying such-and-such, so I said likewise.' A hole will be opened for him, through which he will see Paradise with all its luxuries, and he will be told, 'Look at that which Allah has taken away from you.' Then a hole will be opened for him, through which he will see Hell-fire, parts of it consuming others. He will be told, 'This is your place in it. You used to doubt, you died doubting and you will be resurrected doubting, *in sha' Allah.*' Then he will be punished.' "»[13]

19-For the Believer, a door will be opened from his grave onto Paradise.

---

[13] Narrated by Ahmad, with a *sahih* isnad; reported in *Sahih at-Targhib wa't-Tarhib.*

20- For the *Kâfir*, a door will be opened from his grave onto Hell-fire.

21- The Believer will see his place in Paradise, and the *Kâfir* will see his place in Hell-fire.

22- The grave of the Believer will be widened as far as the eye can see, and the grave of the *Kâfir* will be constricted.

23- The good deeds will come in the form of a handsome, well-dressed, finely-perfumed man, who will bring glad tidings. The bad deeds will come in the form of a scruffily-dressed, stinking man who will bring disturbing news.

24- The *Kâfir* will be struck with an iron chain until he is turned to dust.

This is indicated by the hadith of al-Bara' ibn 'Âzib (رضي الله عنه) who said:

«We went out with the Prophet (ﷺ) to attend the funeral of one of the Ansâri men. When we reached the grave, and before the man was buried, the Messenger of Allah (ﷺ) sat down (facing the *Qiblah*) and we sat down around him. We were as silent and still as if there were birds on our heads, and he had in his hand a stick with which he scratched up the earth. (He began to look up to the sky and down at the ground, and he raised and lowered his gaze three times). He said, "Seek refuge with Allah from the punishment of the grave", two or three times. Then he said, "When the believing slave is

reaching the end of his time in this world, and starting out in the Hereafter, angels with white faces which look like the sun come down to him from Heaven, bringing one of the shrouds of Paradise and some of its *Hunut*[14]. They sit down around him, as far as the eye can see. Then the Angel of Death comes and sits by his head, and says, 'O' good (or secure) soul, come out to the forgiveness and pleasure of Allah.' The narrator said, 'So it will come out like a drop of water coming out of the mouth of a waterskin, and he (the Angel of Death) will take it. (In another report, he said, 'Until when his soul comes out, every angel who is between the heaven and the earth will pray for him, as will every angel in heaven. The gates of heaven will be opened for him, and the people in every level of heaven will pray to Allah to permit his soul to ascend through their domain.')
'When (the Angel of Death) has taken the soul, the (other angels) don't leave it in his hand for a moment; they take it straightaway, wrap it in the shroud and scent it with the *Hunut*. This is what Allah says,

$$﴿وَهُوَ ٱلْقَاهِرُ فَوْقَ عِبَادِهِۦ وَيُرْسِلُ عَلَيْكُمْ حَفَظَةً حَتَّىٰٓ إِذَا جَآءَ أَحَدَكُمُ ٱلْمَوْتُ تَوَفَّتْهُ رُسُلُنَا وَهُمْ لَا يُفَرِّطُونَ ۝﴾$$

[الأنعام: ٦١]

﴿...When death approaches any of you, Our angels take

---

[14] A mixture of good scents used only to scent the shroud and body of the dead.

his soul, and they never fail in their duty.⟩ *(Qur'an 6: 61)*

And there emerges from the soul a scent like the finest musk to be found on the face of the earth.' He said, 'They take the soul up, and whenever they take it past a group of angels, they ask, 'Who is this good soul?', and they reply, 'It is so-and-so, the son of so-and-so' using the best names with which he was addressed in this world. (They go on) until they reach the first heaven; they ask for it to be opened, and it is opened for them. In each heaven, those who are closest to Allah will accompany him to the next heaven, until they reach the seventh heaven, where Allah, may He be exalted and glorified, will say,

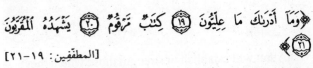

[المطففين: ١٩-٢١]

⟨'Register the book of My slave in *'Illiyûn*, and what will explain to you what *'Illiyûn* is? [There is] a Register [fully] inscribed, to which bear witness those nearest [to Allah].'⟩   *(Qur'an 83: 19-21)*

So his book will be registered in *'Illiyûn*. Then Allah (ﷻ) will say, 'Take him back to the earth, for this was my promise, I created them from it, I will return them to it, and I will resurrect them from it again.' He said, 'He will be taken back to the earth, and his soul will be returned to his body. (He said, 'And he will hear the footsteps of his companions as they leave him'). Two stern angels will come to him, (rebuke him) and sit him up. They will ask him, 'Who is your Lord?' He will answer, 'My Lord is Allah.' They will ask him, 'What is your religion?' He will say, 'My religion is Islam.' They will ask, 'Who is this man who was sent among you?' He will say, 'He is the Messenger of Allah (ﷺ).' They will ask him, 'What did you do?' He will say, 'I read (or recited) the Book of Allah, and I believed in it.' He will rebuke him and ask, 'Who is your Lord? What is your religion? Who is your Prophet?' — This is the last of the trials to face the Believers, as Allah, may He be glorified says,

$$﴿ يُثَبِّتُ ٱللَّهُ ٱلَّذِينَ ءَامَنُوا بِٱلْقَوْلِ ٱلثَّابِتِ فِي ٱلْحَيَوٰةِ ٱلدُّنْيَا وَفِي ٱلْأَخِرَةِ ... ٢٧ ﴾$$

[إبراهيم: ٢٧]

﴾Allah will establish in strength those who believe, with the word that stands firm in this world and in the Hereafter...﴿

(Qur'an 14: 27)

He will say: 'My Lord is Allah, my religion is Islam and my Prophet is Muhammad (ﷺ).' A voice will call from Heaven, 'My slave has spoken the Truth, so furnish his grave from Paradise and clothe him from Paradise, and open for him a gate to Paradise.' He said, 'Some of its breeze and scent will reach him, and his grave will be widened for him as far as the eye can see.' He said, 'There will come to him (or there will appear before him) a handsome, well-dressed and finely-scented man, who will say, 'I bring good news which will make you glad. I bring good news of the good pleasure of Allah, and Gardens wherein is eternal blessing. This is the day which you were promised.' He will say, 'And you, may Allah give you better news. Who are you?' He will say, 'I am your good deeds, and by Allah I only ever saw you hastening to obey Allah, and ever-reluctant to disobey Him, so may Allah reward you with good.' Then a gate of Paradise and a gate of Hell will be opened for him, and it will be said to him, 'This is your place (*Manzil*) if you had disobeyed Allah, but Allah has given you this instead of that.' When he sees what is in Paradise he will say, 'My Lord! Hasten the coming of the Hour, so that I may return to my family and my wealth.' It will be said to him, 'Be patient.' (Literally, 'Dwell here').'

He said, 'As for the disbelieving (lit. corrupt) man, when he leaves this world and enters the Hereafter, stern and harsh angels come down to him from heaven; their faces are black and they bring with them sack-cloth from Hell. They sit around him, as far as the eye can see. The Angel of Death comes and sits at his head, and says, 'O' evil soul, come out to the anger and wrath of Allah!' He said, 'The soul will be dragged out of his body with as much difficulty as a many-pronged skewer being dragged through wet wool (the veins and nerves will be destroyed by it). He will be cursed by every

angel between heaven and earth, and by every angel in
heaven. The gates of heaven will be locked and the
people of every heaven will pray to Allah not to allow
his soul to ascend through their domain. He will take it,
and immediately put it into the sack-cloth; it will stink
like the foulest stench of dead flesh ever witnessed on
earth. They will take the soul up, and whenever they
take it past a group of angels, they will say, 'Who is this
evil soul?' They say, 'It is so-and-so the son of so-and-
so', using the worst names with which he was addressed
in the world. (They will go on) until they reach the first
heaven; they will ask for it to be opened to them, and it
will not be opened. Then the Messenger of Allah (ﷺ)
recited:

﴿ ... لَا تُفَتَّحُ لَهُمْ أَبْوَبُ ٱلسَّمَآءِ وَلَا يَدْخُلُونَ ٱلْجَنَّةَ حَتَّىٰ يَلِجَ ٱلْجَمَلُ
فِى سَمِّ ٱلْخِيَاطِ ... ﴾

[الأعراف : ٤٠]

﴿... No opening will there be of the gates of heaven, nor
will they enter the Garden, until the camel can pass
through the eye of the needle...﴾   *(Qur'an 7: 40)*

Allah, may He be glorified and exalted, will say,
'Register his book in *Sijjin*, in the lowest earth.' Then
Allah will say, 'Take him back to the earth, for this was
my promise. I created them from it, I will return them to
it, and I will resurrect them from it again.' So his soul
will be thrown down from heaven until it reaches his
body. Then he recited,

﴿ ... وَمَن يُشْرِكْ بِاللَّهِ فَكَأَنَّمَا خَرَّ مِنَ ٱلسَّمَآءِ فَتَخْطَفُهُ ٱلطَّيْرُ أَوْ تَهْوِى بِهِ ٱلرِّيحُ فِى مَكَانٍ سَحِيقٍ ٣١ ﴾

[الحَجّ : ٣١]

﴿... If anyone assigns partners to Allah, he is as if he had fallen from heaven and been snatched up by birds, or the wind had swopped [like a bird on its prey] and thrown him into a far-distant place.﴾   *(Qur'an 22: 31)*

So his soul will be returned to his body (he said, 'he will hear the footsteps of his companions when they leave him'). Two stern angels will come to him, rebuke him and sit him up. They will ask him, 'Who is your Lord?' He will say, '*Hah-hah* (indicative of pain or laughter), I do not know!' They will ask him, 'What is your religion?' He will say, '*Hah-Hah*, I do not know.' They will ask, 'What do you say about this man who was sent among you?' He will not even know his name, but he will be told — 'Muhammad' — and he will say, '*Hah-Hah*, I do not know! I heard the people saying such-and-such.' He will be told, 'May you never know!' Then a voice will call from heaven, saying, 'He has lied, so furnish his grave from Hell, and open for him a gate to Hell' — so some of its heat and venom will reach him, and his grave will be constricted until his ribs are crushed together. There will come to him (or there will appear before him) a man with an ugly face, badly-dressed, and foul-smelling. He will say, 'I bring you bad news: this is the day which you were promised.' He will say, 'And you, may Allah give you even worse news! Who are you? Your face brings bad news!' He will say, 'I am your evil deeds. By Allah, I only ever saw you reluctant to obey Allah, and ever-eager to disobey Him. May Allah repay you with evil!' Then there will be sent to him one who is blind, deaf and dumb, who will carry in his hand an iron rod which, if he were to beat a camel with it, would turn it to dust. He will beat him with it until he turns to dust, then Allah will restore him, then he will be beaten again. He will emit a scream which the whole of creation will hear, except for men and Jinn. Then a gate will be opened for him to Hell, and his grave will be furnished from Hell. He will say, 'My Lord, may the Hour never come!'."»

25-The people of heaven will welcome the good soul, and there will be glad tidings for it.

26-There will be no welcome for the evil soul, and only bad tidings for it.

27-The Believer will see the Fire from which Allah has saved him.

28-There will be a little gap through which the evil man will glimpse the Paradise which Allah has denied him.

The Prophet (ﷺ) said:

«The dead person is attended by angels. If he was a righteous man they say, "Come out, O' good soul who was in a good body! Come out praiseworthy, and receive the glad tidings of comfort and sweet scent, and a Lord Who is not angry." They keep on saying this until (the soul) comes out, then they take it up to the heaven, and ask for it to be opened for him. It is asked, 'Who is this?' and they say, 'So-and-so,' so (the inhabitants of heaven) say, 'Welcome to the good soul, who was in a good body; enter praiseworthy and receive the good tidings of comfort and sweet scents, and a Lord who is not angry. And they carry on saying this until they reach the (highest) heaven where Allah, may He be blessed and exalted, is.' And if he was a bad man, they say, 'Come out, O' evil soul! Come out blameworthy, and receive the tidings of a boiling fluid, and a fluid dark, murky, intensely cold!' — and other penalties of a similar kind, to match them! [cf. *(Qur'an 38: 57-58)*]. They keep on saying this until (the soul) comes out, then they take it up to the heaven and ask for it to be opened for it. It is asked, 'Who is this?' They say, 'It is so-and-so.' They say, 'There is no welcome for the evil soul who was in an evil body. Go back blameworthy. The gates of heaven are not opened for you. So (the soul) is sent back from the heaven, and returns to the grave.

The righteous man is sat up in his grave, not scared or terrified. He is asked, 'In what (religion) were you?' He says, 'I was in Islam.' He is asked, 'Who is this man?' He says, 'Muhammad, the Messenger of Allah (ﷺ). He brought us clear signs from Allah and we believed him.'

He is asked, 'Have you seen Allah?' He says, 'No-one may see Allah.' Then he is shown Hell-fire, parts of it consuming others, and he is told, 'Look at that which Allah, may He be exalted, has saved you from.' Then he is shown Paradise, and he looks at its beauty and everything in it.' He is told, 'This is your place.' And he is told, 'You were certain (*'ala'l-Yaqîn*), you died certain, and you will be raised certain, *in sha 'Allah*. The bad man is sat up in his grave, scared and terrified. He is asked, 'In what [religion] were you?' He says, 'I don't know.' He is asked, 'Who is this man?' He says, 'I heard the people saying such-and-such, and I said likewise.' Then he is shown Paradise, and looks at its beauty and everything in it. He is told, 'Look at that which Allah has denied you.' Then he is shown Hell-fire, parts of it consuming others. He is told, 'This is your place. You were in doubt, you died in doubt and you will be raised in doubt, *in sha' Allah*.'"»[15]

29-The angels smell the scent of the soul of the believer.

30-The believers welcome the new soul of a believer with more joy than the family of one who has been absent, on his homecoming.

31-When the soul joins the souls of other believers, it enjoys respite from the grief of this world.

---

[15] Ibn Mâjah. This hadith is also to be found in *Ṣaḥîḥ al-Jâmi'*; hadith no. 1964 by Shaykh al-Albâni, and *at-Targhîb wa't-Tarhîb*.

From Abu Hurayrah (مﷲﻲﺿﺭ), from the Prophet (ﷺ) who said:

«When the believer is taken (by death), angels of mercy
come to him with white silk, and say, 'Come out to the
spirit of Allah.' So (the soul) comes out, like the best
scent of musk. Then the angels pass the soul to one
another, smelling it, until they bring it to the (first)
heaven. They say, 'What is this good scent which has
come from the earth?' In every heaven, the same
question is asked, until they bring him to join the souls
of the believers. They are more overjoyed to welcome
him than the family of one who has been absent, when
he comes home. They ask him, 'What happened to so-
and-so?' They (i.e. the angels who have brought him)
say, 'Leave him to rest, for he has been suffering in the
world.' He says, 'He died, didn't he come to you?' They
(the angels) say, 'He has gone to a place where he will
have his home in a (bottomless) Pit [cf. *(Qur'an 101: 9)*].
As for the *Kâfir*, angels of wrath will come to him with
sackcloth. They say, 'Come out to the wrath of Allah.'
So (the soul) comes out like the foulest stench of dead
meat, and they take it to the gates of the earth.'»[16]

32- The individual in the grave will be shown his place in
Paradise or Hell continuously.

Allah (ﷻ) said:

---

[16] Ibn Hibbân, *Ṣaḥîḥ*, a similar hadith is narrated by Ibn Mâjah with a
ṣaḥîḥ isnad. See Shaykh al-Albâni in *Ṣaḥîḥ at-Targhîb waʾt-Tarhîb*.

﴿النَّارُ يُعْرَضُونَ عَلَيْهَا غُدُوًّا وَعَشِيًّا وَيَوْمَ تَقُومُ السَّاعَةُ أَدْخِلُوٓا۟ ءَالَ

فِرْعَوْنَ أَشَدَّ الْعَذَابِ ﴿٤٦﴾ [غافر : ٤٦]

﴾In front of the Fire will they be brought morning and evening: and [the Sentence will be] on the Day that Judgement will be established: Cast the People of Pharaoh into the severest Penalty!﴿   *(Qur'an 40: 46)*

From Ibn 'Umar (ﷺ): the Messenger of Allah (ﷺ) said:

«When any of you dies, he is shown his place morning and evening. If he is one of the people of Paradise, then he is one of them, and if he is one of the people of Hell, then he is one of them. He is told, "This is your place until Allah raises you on the Day of Resurrection."»[17]

33-The animals can hear the voices of those who are being punished in their graves.

From Ibn Mas'ûd (ﷺ): The Prophet (ﷺ) said:

«The dead are being punished in their graves, and even the animals can hear their voices.»[18]

34- The grave is the first stage of the Hereafter from Hane'a the servant of 'Uthmân ibn Affân (ﷺ) said:

«'Uthmân (ﷺ) used to cry until he wet his beard, if he was to stand on a grave, he was told, "You mention the

---

[17] Bukhari and Muslim.

[18] Classed *ṣaḥîḥ* by Shaykh al-Albani, *Ṣaḥîḥ al-Jâmi'*, hadith no. 1961.

Heaven and the Hell-Fire and you don't cry, but when you mention the grave you burst in tears!" He said, "I heard the Prophet of Allah (ﷺ) saying, 'The grave is the first stage of the Hereafter, whoever passes it will be at ease afterwards, and if he does not pass it he will be in worst of condition.' I also heard him saying, 'Never I saw a sight more horrifying than that of a grave.'"»

35-The graves of those who fell into disobedience will be filled with darkness.

The Prophet (ﷺ) said:

«These graves are filled with darkness for their occupants. Allah enlightens them by my praying for them.»[19]

36-The living are not able to hear the punishment of the grave.

The Prophet (ﷺ) said:

«This Ummah will be tried in its graves. If it were not for the fear that you might not bury your dead, I would pray to Allah to make you hear what I hear.»[20]

37-Food from the trees of Paradise before the Day of Judgement.

The Prophet (ﷺ) said:

«The soul of the believer is a bird eating from the trees

---

[19] Muslim et al.
[20] Muslim, Aḥmad.

of Paradise until Allah restores it to its body on the Day of Resurrection.»[21]

38-The soul of the believer is tied to his debts.

The Prophet (ﷺ) said:

«The soul or the believer is tied to his debts until they are paid off.»[22]

39-The people of heaven pray for the believer.

The Prophet (ﷺ) said:

«When the soul of the believer comes out, two angels receive it and take it up — he (ﷺ) mentioned its good scent — and the people of heaven say, 'It is a good soul, which has come from the earth; may Allah bless you and the body which you occupied.' The soul will be taken up to its Lord, then it will be said, 'Take it to its destiny.'

When the soul of the *Kâfir* comes out — he (ﷺ) mentioned its stench — the people of heaven will say, 'It is an evil soul which has come from the earth.' It is said, 'Take him to his destiny?'»[23]

40-The grave of the believer will be well-lit.

---

[21] Classed as *saḥîḥ* by Shaykh al-Albâni, op. cit, hadith no. 2369.

[22] Narrated and classed as *ḥasan* by Tirmidhi; classed as *saḥîḥ* by Shaykh al-Albâni, op. cit, hadith no. 6655.

[23] Muslim.

41-The believer will sleep in his grave.

42-The deceased will long to tell his family of his good news.

The Messenger of Allah (ﷺ) said:

«When the deceased is buried, two black-and-blue angels come to him, one called *al-Munkar* and the other called *an-Nakir*. They ask, 'What did you use to say about this man?' He will say that what he used to say was, 'He is the slave of Allah and His Messenger, I bear witness that there is no god but Allah, and that Muhammad is His slave and Messenger.' They will say, 'We knew that you would say this.' Then they will expand his grave for him, seventy cubits by seventy, and light it for him. Then he will be told, 'Sleep'. He will say, 'I want to go back to my family and tell them.' They will say, 'Sleep like the groom who should not be woken by any except those he loves most,' — until Allah will resurrect him from his place of rest.

If he was a hypocrite, he will say, 'I heard the people saying such-and-such, and I said likewise. I do not know.' They will say, 'We knew that you would say this.' Then the earth will be told, 'Press him'; so it will press him and his ribs will be crushed together. It will continue to punish him until Allah resurrects him from that place.'»[24]

---

[24] Classed as *ḥasan* by Shaykh al-Albâni, op. cit, hadith no. 737.

43-The grave of the believer will be filled with greenery until the Day of Resurrection.

The Prophet (ﷺ) said:

«When a person is placed in his grave and his companions leave him, he can hear their footsteps. Then two angels come to him, sit him up, and ask him, 'What did you use to say about this man?' i.e. Muhammad. The believer will say, 'I bear witness that he is the slave and Messenger of Allah.' Then he will be told, 'Look at your place in Hell-fire, which Allah has exchanged for a place in Paradise.' So he will look at them both. Then his grave will be widened for him, to a distance of seventy cubits, and it will be filled with greenery until the Day of Resurrection.

The *Kâfir* or hypocrite will be asked, 'What did you used to say about this man?' He will say, 'I don't know. I used to say whatever the people were saying.' He will be told, 'You did not know and you did not care!' Then he will be struck with an iron hammer between his two ears, and will utter a cry which will be heard by every creature around him, except for Jinn and men. Then his grave will be constricted for him until his ribs are crushed.»[25]

44-The answers given by the believer in the grave are the result of guidance from Allah (ﷻ).

---

[25] Bukhari and Muslim.

45-The individual is asked about his worship and religion in the grave.

The Prophet (ﷺ) said:

«When the believer is placed in his grave, an angel comes to him and asks him, 'What did you use to worship?' Allah guides him and he says, 'I used to worship Allah.' He is asked, 'What did you use to say about this man?' He says, 'He is the slave and Messenger of Allah.' He will not be asked about anything else. He is taken to a house which was in the Hell-fire, and he is told, 'This is your house which was in the Hell-fire, but Allah has protected you and had mercy on you, and has exchanged it for a house in Paradise for you.' He asks, 'Let me go and tell my family of this good news', but he is told, 'Remain where you are.' When the *Kâfir* is placed in his grave, an angel comes to him and rebukes him, and asks him, 'What did you use to worship?' He says, 'I don't know.' He is told, 'You didn't know and you didn't care!' He is asked, 'What did you use to say about this man?' He says, 'I used to say whatever the people were saying.' Then he will be struck between the ears with an iron hammer and will utter a cry which will be heard by the whole of creation apart from Jinn and men.»[26]

---

[26] Narrated by Abu Da'wûd from Anas; see *Ṣaḥîḥ al-Jâmi'*, hadith no. 1926.

46-The dead do not hear what is going on earth.

Allah (ﷺ) said:

$$\text{﴿فَإِنَّكَ لَا تُسْمِعُ ٱلْمَوْتَىٰ وَلَا تُسْمِعُ ٱلصُّمَّ ٱلدُّعَآءَ إِذَا وَلَّوْا مُدْبِرِينَ﴾}$$

[الرُّوم: ٥٢]

❴So verily you cannot make the dead to hear, nor can you make the deaf to hear the call, when they show their backs and turn away❵   *(Qur'an 30: 52)*

47-The (dead) people of Kulaib heard the words of the Prophet (ﷺ), but were not able to reply[27].

It is proven in Bukhari that the Prophet (ﷺ) looked upon the dead *Kuffâr* of Kulaib after the Battle of Badr and said:

«Have you found what your Lord promised you to be true? He was asked, 'Are you calling the dead?' He said, 'You do not hear any better than they, but they cannot reply.'»

48-The *Ṣaḥâbah* who had been martyred in the way of Allah (ﷺ) and were in *al-Barzakh* longed to tell their brothers who had not died of the honour which was prepared for the martyrs.

---

[27] This applies only to the dead *Kuffâr* thrown into the well following the Battle of Badr, the general rule is that the dead do not hear. See al-Alusi, *Kitâb al-Âyât al-Bayyinat fî 'Âdam Sama' al-Amwat* (ed. al-Albâni).

The Prophet (ﷺ) said:

«When your brothers were martyred at Uḥud, Allah placed their souls inside green birds which drink from the rivers of Paradise, eat of its fruits and seek shelter in lamps of gold which are suspended in the shade of the Throne. When they saw how good their food, drink and abode were, they said, 'Who will tell our brothers about us, that we are alive in Paradise and being amply provided for, so that they will not turn away from Jihad or abandon war?' Allah, may He be exalted, said, 'I will tell them about you.'»[28]

---

[28] Aḥmad, Abu Da'wûd and al-Ḥâkim. Classed as *ṣaḥîḥ* by Shaykh al-Albâni, op. cit, hadith no. 5081.

PART FOUR

The Physical Punishment of Sinners in the Grave

Samurah ibn Jundub reported that the Messenger of Allah (ﷺ) often used to ask his Companions:

«"Has any one of you seen a dream?" So whoever Allah wished to do so would tell of a dream he had seen. One morning, he told us, "Last night, two persons came to me (in a dream), and said to me, 'Let's go!'
So I set off with them, and we came to a man who was lying down, with another man standing over him holding a big rock. He was throwing the rock down on the other man's head, smashing it. The rock rolled away, and the thrower went after it and brought it back. By the time he came back to the man, his head has been restored, then he proceeded to do the same thing again. I said, '*Subhân-Allâh*! Who are these two?' (My two companions) said to me, 'Go on, go on!'
So we went on, and came to a man lying flat on his back, with another man standing over him holding and iron hook. He put the hook in one side of the man's

mouth and tore off that side of his face to the back (of his neck), and then tear his nose likewise from front to back, and his eye from front to back, and then do the same on the other side of the man's face. He had hardly finished on the second side, when the first side was restored, so he went back and started again. I said, '*Subḥân-Allâh*! Who are these two?' (My two companions) said, 'Go on, go on!'

So we went on, and came across something like a *Tannur* (a kind of oven: usually a pit lined with clay for baking bread). — I think he said, 'In it there was much noise and voices.' — We looked into it, and inside it were naked men and women, with flames coming up to them from underneath; When the flames reached them, they cried loudly. I asked, 'Who are these?' (My two companions) said, 'Go on, go on!'

So we went on and came to a river — I think he said, 'Red like blood' — and in the river there was a man swimming, and another man on the bank who had gathered many stones. The man who was swimming came to the one who had gathered many stones, and opened his mouth, and the man on the river-bank placed a stone in his mouth. The man in the river swam away, then came back, and every time he came back, he opened his mouth and a stone was put in it. I asked (my two companions), 'Who are these two?' and they said to me, 'Go on, go on!'

So we went on, and came to an ugly man, with the most

repulsive appearance you have ever seen. Beside him was a fire, and he was kindling it and running around it. I asked, 'Who is this?' (My two companions) said to me, 'Go on, go on!'

So we went on, and came to a garden of deep green dense vegetation, with all sorts of spring colours. In the midst of the garden there was a very tall man, so tall that I could hardly see his head. Around this man were more children than I had ever seen. I asked, 'Who is this? Who are they?' (My two companions) said, 'Go on, go on!' So we went on until we came to a huge garden, bigger and more magnificent than any I have ever seen. (My two companions) told me, 'Go up into it', so we went up into it, to a city built of gold and silver bricks. We came to the gate of the city, asked for it to be opened, and we were admitted. There we met men with one half of their bodies as handsome as any you have ever seen, and the other half as ugly. (My two companions) told them, 'Go and throw yourselves into that river' — there was a river flowing through the city, with water as white as milk. They went and did as they were ordered, and came back with all trace of ugliness removed, in the best form. (My two companions) told me, 'This is the Paradise of *'Adan* (*Jannah 'Adan* — Garden of Eden), and that is your place' — and I looked up and saw a palace like white clouds! (My two companions) said to me, 'That is your place.' I said to them, 'May Allah bless you both! Let me enter it. They said, 'Now (is not the time) for you to enter it.' I said, 'I have seen many wonders tonight. What is (the meaning of) all that I have seen?' They said, 'We will inform you: The first man whom you saw having his head smashed with a rock, is the man who studies the Qur'an but neither recites nor acts upon it, and who sleeps and neglects the prescribed prayers. The man you saw having his face torn from his mouth, nose and eyes, front to back, is the man who goes out of his house in the morning and tells so many lies that it spreads all over the world. The naked men and women who were in something like a *Tannur* are the adulterers and adulteresses, and the man whom you saw swimming in the river and having stones thrown in his mouth was one who used to consume *Riba* (usury). The ugly-looking man you saw kindling the fire and walking around it is Mâlik, the gatekeeper of Hell. The tall man in the garden is Ibrahîm, and the children around him are all the children who died in a state of *fiṭrah* (i.e. the natural-born state of mankind).

Some of the Muslims asked, 'O' Messenger of Allah! What about the children of the *Mushrikîn* [pagans]?' The Messenger of Allah (ﷺ) said, 'The children of *Mushrikîn* (are there) too. And the people who appeared half handsome and half ugly were those who had mixed a good deed with a bad deed, but Allah forgave them.' "»[29]

---

[29] Bukhari.

In another report:

«Tonight I saw (in a dream) two men who came to me and took me to a holy land. Then he mentioned it and said, "We went on and came to a hole like a *Tannur*. Its upper part was narrow and its lower part was wide. The bottom of it was filled with fire. When the fire flared up, it lifted up the people inside, so that they nearly came out of the top, and when the fire died down, they went back inside. In this hole were naked men and women. We went on until we came to a river of blood — a man was standing in the middle of this river, and on the bank there was a man who had some stones in front of him. The man in the river would approach him, but when he tried to climb out, the man on the bank put a stone in his mouth, and pushed him back. Every time the man in the river tried to come out, the one on the bank threw a stone in his mouth and sent him back... They brought me to a tree and took me into a house more beautiful than any I have ever seen, in which there were old men and young men.. The one whom I saw with his mouth being torn, was the liar who spoke lies which spread from him until it reached the horizon; they will continue doing this to him until the Day of Resurrection... The one whom I saw with his head being smashed is the one whom Allah taught the Qur'an, but he slept (and failed to recite it) at night, and failed to act upon it during the day; they will continue doing this to him until the Day of Resurrection. The first house which I entered is a house for all the believers, and the (second) house is the house of the martyrs... 'I am Jibrîl and this is Mika'il. Look up!' So I looked up and above me I saw something like clouds. They said, 'That is your place.' I asked, 'Let me enter my place.' They said, 'There is still some time for you to complete; when you have completed it you will come to your place.'"»[30]

[30] Narrated by Bukhari; quoted from an-Nawawi, *Riyadh aṣ-Ṣaliḥîn, Bâb Taḥrîm al-Kadhb*.

PART FIVE

The Sins for Which the Sinners will be Punished in the Grave

1-Punishment for the one who learnt the Qur'an and refused to act upon it, and for sleeping through the prescribed prayers.

We have already quoted the hadith of Samurah ibn Jundub in full. It includes the words:

«... We came to a man who was lying down, with another man standing over him holding a big rock. He was throwing the rock down on the other man's head, smashing it. The rock rolled away, and the thrower went after it and brought it back. By the time he came back to the man, his head has been restored, then he proceeded to do the same thing again...»

At the end of the hadith, the two angels told the Messenger of Allah (ﷺ):

«... The first man whom you saw having his head smashed with a rock, is the man who studies the Qur'an but neither recites nor acts upon it, and who sleeps and neglects the prescribed prayers.»

In another report it was said:

«They will carry on doing that to him until the Day of
Resurrection.»

2-Punishment for Lying

In the hadith of Samurah ibn Jundub, it also says:

«... So we went on, and came to a man lying flat on his
back, with another man standing over him holding an
iron hook. He put the hook in one side of the man's
mouth and tore off that side of his face to the back (of
his neck), and then tear his nose likewise from front to
back, and his eye from front to back, and then do the
same on the other side of the man's face. He had hardly
finished on the second side, when the first side was
restored, so he went back and started again.»

And at the end of the hadith:

«... The man you saw having his face torn from his
mouth, nose and eyes, front to back, is the man who
goes out of his house in the morning and tells so many
lies that it spreads all over the world.»

And in another report it is said:

«They will carry on doing that to him until the Day of
Resurrection.»

3-Punishment for adulterers and adulteresses.

The hadith quoted above also says:

«So we went on, and came across something like a *Tannur* (a kind of oven: usually a pit lined with clay for baking bread). — I think he said, 'In it there was much noise and voices.' — We looked into it, and inside it were naked men and women, with flames were coming up to them from underneath; when the flames reached them, they cried loudly.»

This is explained as follows:

«The naked men and women who were in something like a *Tannur* are the adulterers and adulteresses.»

4-Punishment for consuming *Riba* (usury).

Also mentioned in the Hadith quoted:

«... So we went on and came to a river — I think he said, 'Red like blood' — and in the river there was a man swimming, and another man on the bank who had gathered many stones. The man who was swimming came to the one who had gathered many stones, and opened his mouth, and the man on the river-bank placed a stone in his mouth. The man in the river swam away, then came back, and everytime he came back, he opened his mouth and a stone was put in it.»

At the end of the hadith:

«... and the man whom you saw swimming in the river and having stones thrown in his mouth was one who used to consume *Riba* (usury).»

5-Punishment for not cleaning oneself properly after urinating.

The Prophet (صلى الله عليه وسلم) said:

«Most of the punishment in the grave is because of (failing to clean oneself properly after) urinating.»[31]

6-The *Kâfir*'s punishment is increased because of some of his family's weeping for him.

The Prophet (صلى الله عليه وسلم) said:

«Allah increases the punishment of the *Kâfir* by some of his family's weeping for him.»[32]

7-The deceased is punished by (the mourners) wailing for him.

The Prophet (صلى الله عليه وسلم) said:

«The deceased is punished in the grave by (the mourners) wailing for him.»[33]

8-The deceased will be punished because of some of what his family say about him.

---

[31] Classed *sahîh* by Shaykh al-Albâni, *Sahîh al-Jâmi'*, hadith no. 3866.

[32] Nisâ'i; classed as *sahîh* by Shaykh al-Albâni, op. cit., hadith no. 1893.

[33] Bukhari, Muslim, et al. If the deceased had told his family not to wail for him, then he will not be punished; and Allah knows best. See *Ahkâm al-Janâ'iz*, Pp. 28, 29.

The Prophet (ﷺ) said:

«There is no person who dies, and whose mourners begin to cry, 'O' my mountain'! O, my support!' but two angels will be assigned to take care of him. They will strike him and ask, 'Were you really like this!?»[34]

9-Punishment of the one who used to go around spreading slander.

From Ibn 'Abbâs (ﷺ): The Messenger of Allah (ﷺ) passed by two graves and said:

«Truly they are being punished. They are being punished for something which is easily-avoided, but is a major sin if it is committed. One of them used to go around spreading slander, and the other used to neglect to clean himself after urinating.»[35]

---

[34] Tirmidhi. Classed as *ṣaḥîḥ* by Shaykh al-Albâni, op. cit.,, hadith no. 5664. See also *at-Targhîb wa't-Tarhîb*.

[35] Bukhari and Muslim.

PART SIX

The Prophets and *Barzakh*

1-Allah, may He be exalted, has assigned an angel to the grave of the Prophet (ﷺ), to inform him of those who send blessings on him by telling him the name of the person who has sent blessings on the Messenger (ﷺ).

He (ﷺ) said:

«Increase the blessings you send on me, for Allah has assigned an angel to my grave. Whenever anyone of my Ummah sends blessings on me, that angel will say to me, 'O' Muhammad, so-and-so the son of so-and-so has sent blessings on you now.»[36]

He (ﷺ) said:

«Increase the blessings you send on me on Fridays, for every time someone sends blessings and prays for me on a Friday, I will be told about his prayer...»[37]

---

[36] Ad-Daylami, *Musnad al-Firdaws*; classed as *hasan* by Shaykh al-Albâni in *Ṣaḥîḥ al-Jâmi'*, hadith no. 1218.

[37] Classed as *ṣaḥîḥ* by Shaykh al-Albâni, op. cit, hadith no. 1219.

2-The earth does not consume the bodies of the Prophets.

The Prophets (ﷺ) said:

«The best of your days is Friday. Âdam was created on a
Friday and died on a Friday; the Trumpet will be blown
on a Friday, and all the living will be struck down on a
Friday. Increase the blessings you send on me on
Fridays, for I will be told about your prayers. Allah has
forbidden the earth to consume the bodies of the
Prophets.»[38]

3-The Prophets are alive in the grave.

4-They, peace be upon them, pray in their graves.

The Prophet (ﷺ) said:

«The Prophets are alive in their graves, and pray[39]... On
the night of the *Isra'* [Night Journey], I passed by Mûsa
(who was) standing in his grave and praying.»[40]

5-The Messenger (ﷺ) met Âdam, Yaḥyâ, 'Eesa, Yusuf, Idrîs,
Harûn, Mûsa and Ibrahîm (ﷺ).

6-Mûsa (ﷺ) wept in *Barzakh* out of jealousy (NB: the Arabic
word used here refers specifically to a positive form of
jealousy and is not to be taken to have a negative
connotation).

---

[38] Abu Da'wûd, Nisâ'i. Ibn Mâjah, et al. See also Shaykh al-Albâni,
op. cit, hadith no. 2208.

[39] Classed as *Ṣaḥîḥ* by Shaykh al-Albâni, op. cit, hadith no. 2787.

[40] Muslim, et al.

7-Mûsa (﷽) advised our Prophet (﷽) to ask Allah, may He be exalted, to reduce the (number of) obligatory prayers.

From Mâlik ibn Sa'sa'ah (﷽) from the Messenger of Allah (﷽) who said:

«While I was lying down in al-Ḥâtim, someone came to me and split open what is between this and this — he indicated the space from the top of his chest to below his navel — and he took out my heart. Then a golden cup filled with faith was brought to me. My heart was washed with Zamzam water, filled up (with faith) and put back in its place. A white beast, smaller than a mule, and bigger than a donkey, called *al-Burâq*, was brought to me. One stride of this creature covered a distance as far as it could see. I was mounted upon it. Jibrîl set off with me until we reached the first heaven, and he asked for it to be opened. He was asked, 'Who is there?' He said, 'Jibrîl'. The voice asked, 'Who is with you?' He said, 'Muhammad'. The voice asked, 'Has revelation been sent to him?' Jibrîl answered, 'Yes'. The voice said, 'Welcome to him, blessed is the one who has come.' — and the first heaven was opened. When I entered, there was Âdam. Jibrîl said, 'This is your father Âdam; greet him.' I greeted him and he returned the greeting, then he said, 'Welcome to the righteous son and the righteous Prophet.'

Then Jibrîl took me up until we reached the second heaven, and he asked for it to be opened. He was asked,

'Who is there?' He said, 'Jibrîl'. The voice asked, 'Who is with you?' He said, 'Muhammad'. The voice asked, 'Has revelation been sent to him?' Jibrîl answered, 'Yes'. The voice said, 'Welcome to him, blessed is the one who has come.' — and the second heaven was opened. When I entered, there were Yaḥya and 'Eesa, who were maternal cousins. Jibrîl said, 'These are Yaḥya and 'Eesa; greet them.' I greeted them and they returned the greeting, then they said, 'Welcome to the righteous brother and the righteous Prophet.'

Then Jibrîl took me up until we reached the third heaven, and he asked for it to be opened. He was asked, 'Who is there?' He said, 'Jibrîl'. The voice asked, 'Who is with you?' He said, 'Muhammad'. The voice asked, 'Has revelation been sent to him?' Jibrîl answered, 'Yes'. The voice said, 'Welcome to him, blessed is the one who has come.' — and the third heaven was opened. When I entered, there was Yusuf. Jibrîl said, 'This is Yusuf, greet him.' I greeted him and he returned the greeting, then he said, 'Welcome to the righteous brother and the righteous Prophet.'

Then Jibrîl took me up until we reached the fourth heaven, and he asked for it to be opened. He was asked, 'Who is there?' He said, 'Jibrîl'. The voice asked, 'Who is with you?' He said, 'Muhammad'. The voice asked, 'Has revelation been sent to him?' Jibrîl answered, 'Yes'. The voice said, 'Welcome to him, blessed is the one who has come.' — and the fourth heaven was opened. When I entered, there was Idrîs. Jibrîl said, 'This is Idrîs; greet him.' I greeted him and he returned the greeting, then he said, 'Welcome to the righteous brother and the righteous Prophet.'

Then Jibrîl took me up until we reached the fifth heaven, and he asked for it to be opened. He was asked, 'Who is there?' He said, 'Jibrîl'. The voice asked, 'Who is with you?' He said, 'Muhammad'. The voice asked, 'Has revelation been sent to him?' Jibrîl answered, 'Yes'. The voice said, 'Welcome to him, blessed is the one who has come.' — and the fifth heaven was opened. When I entered, there was Harûn. Jibrîl said, 'This is Harûn; greet him.' I greeted him and he returned the greeting, then he said, 'Welcome to the righteous brother and the righteous Prophet.'

Then Jibrîl took me up until we reached the sixth heaven, and he asked for it to be opened. He was asked, 'Who is there?' He said, 'Jibrîl'. The voice asked, 'Who is with you?' He said, 'Muhammad'. The voice asked, 'Has revelation been sent to him?' Jibrîl answered, 'Yes'. The voice said, 'Welcome to him, blessed is the one who has come.' — and the sixth heaven was opened. When I entered, there was Mûsa. Jibrîl said, 'This is Mûsa; greet him.' I greeted him and he returned the greeting, then he said, 'Welcome to the righteous brother and the righteous Prophet.'

Then Jibrîl took me up until we reached the seventh heaven, and he asked for it to be opened. He was asked,

'Who is there?'. He said, 'Jibrîl'. The voice asked, 'Who is with you?' He said, 'Muhammad'. The voice asked, 'Has revelation been sent to him?' Jibrîl answered, 'Yes'. The voice said, 'Welcome to him, blessed is the one who has come.' — and the seventh heaven was opened. When I entered, there was Ibrahîm. Jibrîl said, 'This is your father Ibrahîm; great him.' I greeted him and he returned the greeting, then he said, 'Welcome to the righteous son and the righteous Prophet.'

Then I was taken up to the Lote-tree beyond which none may pass [cf. *(Qur'an 53: 14)*]; its fruits were like the pitchers of Hajar and its leaves were like the ears of elephants. Jibrîl said, 'This is the Lote-tree beyond which none may pass.' There were four rivers, two hidden and two visible. I asked, 'What are these, O' Jibrîl?' He said, 'The two hidden rivers are rivers of Paradise; the two visible rivers are the Nile and the Euphrates.'

Then I was taken up to the Much-Frequented Fane [cf. *(Qur'an 52:4)*]. I asked, 'O' Jibrîl, what is this?' He said, 'This is the Much-Frequented Fane; every day, seventy thousand angels pray in it, and when they leave, another seventy thousand come.'

Then I was presented with a vessel of wine, a vessel of milk and a vessel of honey. I chose the milk, and Jibrîl said, 'This is the natural disposition *(Fiṭrah)* of your Ummah.'

Then *Ṣalâh* (Prayer) was made obligatory: fifty prayers every day. Then I returned, and passed by Mûsa, who asked, 'What have you been commanded to do?' I said, 'I have been commanded to perform fifty prayers every day.' He said, 'Your Ummah will not be able to perform fifty prayers every day. By Allah, I tested the people before you, and I tried my utmost to reform the people of Israel. Go back to your Lord and ask Him to lighten the burden of your Ummah.' So I went back, and the number of prayers was reduced by ten (to forty). I went back to Mûsa, and he said the same as before. So I went back, and the number of prayers was reduced by a further ten (to thirty). I went back to Mûsa, and he said the same as before. So I went back again, and the number of prayers was reduced by a further ten (to twenty). I went back to Mûsa, and he said the same as before. So I went back, and the number of prayers was reduced by a further ten (to ten). So I went back to Mûsa, and he said the same as before. So I went back, and was ordered to perform five prayers every day. I came back to Mûsa, and he asked, 'What have you been commanded to do?' I said, 'I have been commanded to perform five prayers every day.' Mûsa said, 'Your Ummah will not be able to perform five prayers every day. I have tested the people before you, and I tried my utmost to reform the people of Israel. Go back to your Lord and ask Him to lighten the burden of your Ummah.' I said, 'I have asked my Lord until I felt

ashamed. Now I am content and submit (to His Will).'
When I passed by, a voice proclaimed, 'I have
confirmed My command and lightened the burden of
My servants'."»[41]

[41] Bukhari, Muslim, Aḥmad and Nisâ'i.

PART SEVEN

Deeds which will Benefit the Deceased after his Death

1-Praying for him.

The Prophet (ﷺ) said.

> «If a company of Muslims numbering one hundred pray over a dead person, all of them interceding for him, their intercession (i.e. prayers for forgiveness and mercy) for him will be accepted.»[42]

> «If a company of the people pray over a dead person, they will intercede for him.»[43]

2- The deceased feels the comforting presence of his brothers in Allah (ﷺ) after the burial, for a period of time equal to the time taken to sacrifice a camel and distribute its meat.·

As quoted before, 'Amr ibn al-'Âṣ (ﷺ) said:

---

[42] Muslim. et al.

[43] Nisâ'i, classed as *ḥasan* by Shaykh al-Albâni in *Ṣaḥîḥ al-Jâmi'*, hadith no. 5663.

«When you bury me, stay around my grave for the time it would take to sacrifice a camel and distribute its meat, so that I may be comforted by your presence, until I see how I will answer the messengers of my Lord.»[44]

3-Praying for strength and forgiveness for him immediately after his burial.

From 'Uthmân ibn Affân (ﷺ) who said:

«Whenever the Prophet (ﷺ) had finished burying anyone, he would stand by the grave and say, 'Ask for forgiveness and strength for your brother, for even now he is being questioned.»[45]

4-Continuous charity *(Ṣadaqah Jâriyah)*, which he set up in his lifetime; beneficial knowledge; and a pious son who will pray for him.

The Prophet (ﷺ) said:

«When a person dies, his deeds stop, except for three: continuous charity, knowledge which benefits others, or a pious son who will pray for him.»[46]

5-Charity given by the son of the deceased on his\her behalf.

'Â'ishah (ﷺ) reported that a man said to the Prophet (ﷺ):

---

[44] Muslim.

[45] Abu Da'wûd; classed as *ṣaḥîḥ* by Shaykh al-Albâni, op. cit, hadith no. 956.

[46] Muslim.

«"My mother died suddenly without making any will. I think she would definitely have given charity *(Ṣadaqah)* if she had been able to speak. Would she have a reward if I gave charity on her behalf?" He said, "Yes."»[47]

6-All the believers and Muslims should pray for him and ask forgiveness for him.

Allah (ﷻ) says:

$$\text{﴿وَٱلَّذِينَ جَآءُو مِنۢ بَعْدِهِمْ يَقُولُونَ رَبَّنَا ٱغْفِرْ لَنَا وَلِإِخْوَٰنِنَا ٱلَّذِينَ سَبَقُونَا بِٱلْإِيمَـٰنِ ... ﴾ [الحشر: ١٠]}$$

◄And those who came after them say, 'Our Lord! Forgive us, and our brethren who came before us into the Faith...►   *(Qur'an 59: 10)*

The Prophet (ﷺ) said:

«Whoever prays for forgiveness for the believing men and believing women, Allah will give him one reward for each believing man and believing women (he prayed for).»[48]

7-Defending the borders of Islam for the sake of Allah (ﷻ) in this world.

The Prophet (ﷺ) said:

---

[47] Bukhari and Muslim.

[48] Ṭabarâni, *al-Kabîr*, classed as *ḥasan* by Shaykh al-Albâni, op. cit., hadith no. 5902.

«When a person dies his good deeds come to an end, except for his defending the borders of Islam for the sake of Allah *(fi sabî lillâh)*. This deed will grow (i.e. in reward) until the Day of Judgement, and he will be protected from the *Fitnah* of the grave.»[49]

---

[49] Abu Da'wûd and Tirmidhi. Described by the latter as a *ṣaḥîḥ ḥasan* hadith.

PART EIGHT

Things Which will Save a Person from the Punishment of the Grave

1-Martyrdom on the battlefield.

1.a. The Prophet (ﷺ) said:

«The martyr enjoys six specific blessings from Allah: his sins will be forgiven from the first moment his blood is shed; he will see his place in Paradise; he will be protected from the punishment of the grave; he will feel secure on the most fearful Day (i.e. the Day of Judgement); he will be clothed in the robes of faith; he will be married to *al-Hûr al-'Ayn*; he will be able to intercede for seventy members of his family.»[50]

1.b. From a man from among the Companions of the Prophet:

«A man asked the Prophet (ﷺ), "O' Messenger of Allah! Why will all the believers except the martyr

---

[50] Tirmidhi reported it and classed it as *ṣaḥîḥ*; also reported by Ibn Mâjah and Aḥmad. Classed as *ṣaḥîḥ* by Shaykh al-Albâni in *Aḥkâm al-Janâ'iz*, Pp. 35-36.

suffer the *Fitnah* of the grave?" He said, "The shining swords above the head of the martyr are *Fitnah* enough!»[51]

2-Defending the borders of Islam for the sake of Allah (ﷻ).

2.a. The Prophet (ﷺ) said:

«Defending the borders of Islam for a day and a night is better than fasting and praying at night for a month; if a man dies (whilst defending the borders of Islam), the good deed he was doing will continue to accumulate reward and bring him sustenance *(Rizq)*, and he will be protected from the *Fitnah* of the grave». [Muslim].

2.b. The Prophet (ﷺ) said:

«When a person dies, his good deeds come to an end, except for his defending the borders of Islam for the sake of Allah *(fī sabî lillâh)*. This deed will grow (i.e. in reward) until the Day of Judgement, and he will be protected from the *Fitnah* of the grave.»

3-Death from a stomach disease.

From 'Abdullah ibn Yassar who said:

«I was sitting with Sulaymân ibn Sard and Khâlid ibn 'Arfatah, and they mentioned that a man had died, from a stomach disease. They expressed their wish to be present at his funeral, and one of them said to the other,

---

[51] Nisâ'i. Classed as *sahîh* by Shaykh al-Albâni, op. cit, p. 36.

"Didn't the Messenger of Allah (ﷺ) say, 'Whoever is killed by a stomach disease will not be punished in the grave?' The other said, 'Yes, indeed'."

In another report: "You have spoken the truth."[52]

4-Reciting *Sûrah Tabâraka* (i.e. Qur'an 67).

The Prophet (ﷺ) said:

«*Sûrah Tabaraka* is a shield from the punishment of the grave.»[53]

5-Dying on a Friday (day or night).

The Prophet (ﷺ) said:

«There is no-one who died on the day or night of Friday, but Allah, may He be exalted, protected him from the *Fitnah* of the grave.»[54]

---

footnotes[52] Classed as *ṣaḥîḥ* by Shaykh al-Albâni, as *ḥasan* by Tirmidhi et al. Classed as *ṣaḥîḥ* in *Aḥkâm al-Janâ'iz*, p. 38.

[53] Classed as *ṣaḥîḥ* by Shaykh al-Albâni in *Ṣaḥîḥ al-Jâmi'*, hadith no. 3537.

[54] Aḥmad, *Musnad* and Tirmidhi. Classed as *ḥasan* by Shaykh al-Albâni, op. cit, hadith no. 5649.

EPILOGUE

Daily Islamic Life

* Do you pray *Fajr* in the mosque every day, in congregation?

* Do you observe every prayer in the mosque in congregation?

* Have you read any part of the Book of Allah today?

* After every prayer, do you recite *Dhikr* and *Wird*?

* Do you observe the regular Sunnah prayers before and after the *Fard* prayers?

* Did you concentrate on your prayer today and really think about the words you were saying?

* Did you remember death and the grave?

* Did you remember the Last Day and its terrors?

* Did you ask Allah (ﷻ) three times to admit you to Paradise?

For whoever asks Allah (ﷺ) to admit him to Paradise, Paradise says: «O' Allah, admit him to Paradise!»[55]

* Have you asked Allah (ﷺ) three times to protect you from the punishment of Hell? Whoever does that, Hell says:

«O' Allah, protect him from Hell!»[56]

* Have you read anything from the hadith of the Prophet (ﷺ)?

* Have you thought of distancing yourself from bad gatherings?

* Have you tried to avoid laughing and joking excessively?

* Have you wept today for fear of Allah (ﷺ)?

* Have you recited the *Dhikr* for morning and evening?

* Have you asked Allah (ﷺ) for forgiveness for your sins today?

---

[55] The hadith in full reads:

«Whoever asks Allah three times for Paradise, Paradise says, "O' Allah! Admit him to Paradise!" And whoever asks three times for protection from Hell, Hell says, "O' Allah! Protect him from Hell!»
Tirmidhi; classed as *ṣaḥīḥ* by Shaykh al-Albâni in *Ṣaḥīḥ al-Jâmi'*, vol. 6, hadith no. 6151.

[56] Ibid.

* Have you asked Allah (ﷻ) sincerely for martyrdom? For the Messenger of Allah (ﷺ) said:

«Whoever asks Allah sincerely for martyrdom, Allah will give him the status of martyr, even if he dies on his bed.»[57]

* Have you asked Allah (ﷻ) to make your heart strong in faith?

* Have you made the most of the hours during which especially Allah (ﷻ) will answer your prayers?

* Have you bought a new Islamic book from which you will learn more about your religion?

* Have you asked forgiveness for the believers, men and women — because for every believing man and believing woman (for whom you ask forgiveness), there will be a reward?

* Have you praised Allah (ﷻ) for the blessing of Islam?

* Have you praised Allah (ﷻ) for the blessing of hearing, sights, reason and all his blessings?

* Have you given charity today to the poor and needy?

---

[57] Muslim, et al.

* Have you refrained from getting angry for your own sake, and only got angry for the sake of Allah (ﷺ)?

* Have you avoided being proud and arrogant?

* Have you visited any of your brothers in Allah (ﷺ)?

* Have you prayed to Allah (ﷺ) for your brothers and neighbours, and anyone else you are in touch with?

* Have you treated your parents with love and kindness?

* Have you responded to any calamity by saying: *Inna Lillâhi wa inna ilayhi Râji'ûn*:

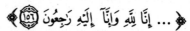

[البَقَرَة: ١٥٦]   ﴿ ... إِنَّا لِلَّهِ وَإِنَّآ إِلَيْهِ رَٰجِعُونَ ١٥٦ ﴾

﴿... To Allah we belong, and to Him is our return.﴾
(Qur'an 2: 156)[58]

* Have you prayed this *Du'â'* today?

"Allâhumma inni a'udhu bika 'an-nushrika bika wa ana

---

[58] The Prophet (ﷺ) said:

«Any one of you should say, *Inna Lillâhi wa inna ilayhi Râji'ûn*, when any misfortune befalls him, even if his shoe gets damaged, for these are all types of 'calamity'.»

Classed as *ḥasan* by Shaykh al-Albâni, *al-Kalim at-Tayyib*, hadith no. 140.

a'lam, wa astaghfiruka lima la a'lam — O' Allah, I
seek refuge with You from knowingly association
anything with You, and ask Your forgiveness if I have
unwittingly done so."

— For whoever says this, Allah (![]) will remove from him
both major and minor forms of *shirk*.[59]

May Allah forgive all our sins and bestow on us His
mercy by saving us from the *fitnah* of the punishment of the
grave and bestow on us His blessings in it, *Amîn*.

****

---

[59] See *Ṣaḥîḥ al-Jâmi'*, hadith no. 3625.

NOTES

....

....

....

....

....

....

....

....

....

....

NOTES

NOTES